Past and Future Versions of th.
A Collection of Poetry from an Addict in Recovery
Amanda Lynn Simons

This book is dedicated to each and every person who helped me see what I was capable of, contributed to my success in small and simple ways, and who inspired me believe in myself.

Thank You.

Forward: I am an Addict. I believe that our stories, as Addicts, should be told, and that telling them may inspire others. My hope is that others won't follow in my footsteps, to never become an Addict, by never using. Addiction is a path that not even those in recovery want to take again. I also hope to inspire those who have chosen to travel down this path, to find help, inspiration, and guidance, and to join me in recovery. Please be warned, this poetry is real; it's raw and emotional. Like addiction itself, this poetry is vulgar, depictive, and at times brutal. It may trigger some of you; it may make you cry, cringe, or scream. That is the point. My hope is that by being completely real and not leaving out a single emotion, you will get a more accurate idea of what my life: past, present, and future is really like.

-Amanda Lynn

My name is Amanda Lynn, and I am an Addict.

I was born in 1982, as I finish this book of poetry, I am 34 years old. I am the survivor of too many abusive situations. I am the mother to 3 complicated and amazing children. I am the wife of a wonderful man who is an amazing step-father to our children. I am an Aries. I am an aspiring writer and an avid reader. I am a movie buff. I am a Mormon (LDS). And I am an addict. And that's the simple and complex truth. I made a choice when I was a teenager, and that choice will stay with me. Always. I live with the consequences of that choice every single day. My story is much like others, filled with abuse, anxiety, and emotional trauma. I used those things as my excuses and kept repeating the same patterns. At times I was convinced that I had everything under control, and other times I realized how little control I had over the things that were happening in my life, all because of the choices I kept making to use drugs. I swapped one drug for another, and even when I wasn't using drugs I was still swapping one addiction for another. My biggest realization came when I understood just how long I had been an addict. I had only used Meth for a few years this time, for the 3rd time in my life, and really, that was no big deal.. Until I had that realization- that wake up call, that sudden clarity- that for years, since I was a teenager and drank alcohol with my friends for the first time. I had consistently been using *something* to numb my emotional pain, for damn near most of my life. Alcohol, Weed, Meth, Cocaine, Opiates, Barbiturates, and more I'm sure I don't remember. Even when that something was food, sex, and compulsive shopping, I was using something to numb my pain. Something besides me was controlling my life. I'm still not perfect.

But I am much more in control of my future right now, than I have ever been. I plan to keep it that way; I plan to continue improving and recovering for the rest of my life. To do this I know that I need to remember what it was like, the desperation I felt when I was using; the ugliness that was my life. I need to work through my fears in order for my recovery to continue to get a bit easier, day by day. Writing these poems has been that release for me. It's been insanely difficult, and sometimes I wanted to give up, but tapping into those feelings, the moments from my past, and the triggers I still feel to this day, has helped me to explore those feelings, work through them, and understand myself a little more each time. I hope that you will hear my story in my poems, understand what the path I took looked like, from each of my points of view: from the beginning of my downward spiral, through all the ups and downs, my active addictions, and finally, through clear eyes as an addict in active recovery.

My name is Amanda Lynn,

and I am a fucking warrior.

Poems by Amanda Lynn

This first poem was written to a friend of mine to celebrate her success in her recovery. It is important to note that she is the one who inspired me to write these poems. I didn't know all that would come from that day, but I am forever grateful to her. She helped me walk farther down the path of recovery without even knowing it.

"Acey Tia, Warrior"

by: Amanda Lynn 05/13/2016

Check you out Acey!!
Look where you're standing,
Your path of destruction WAY behind you
Now surrounded by a life you're commanding!

Picking UP the pieces
And FIXING what you've shattered
Making amends
To the ONE PERSON who ACTUALLY mattered.

Finding the pieces of your former life,
Gathering ALL the skills you'll need
To live a more BEAUTIFUL LIFE this time
Creating a brand new you is your CREED.

THIS TIME you'll be marching FORWARD
Beating your drum to a brand new beat.
Yelling out your WAR CRY!!
Never will you grant defeat.

No longer consumed by doubt,

Your infinite worth you're beginning to see.
Picking up those pieces that lead you
To the BEST version of yourself you can be.

Always believe in the WARRIOR inside you.
Like a BOSS you know you can handle this shit!
WAKE UP. KICK ASS. AND ALWAYS REPEAT,
Relentlessly and forever to this anthem commit!

"Denying My Faith in God"
by Amanda Lynn 05/19/2016

I rebelled from my church as a teenager
confused by things I refused to understand
denying everything I knew
searching for something better
someone, some higher power
to take away my pain.
I felt that everyone in the church
was like him..
Not one person in the church could be trusted
--they would all destroy me
as he had destroyed me.
I felt forgotten
I felt lost
I felt like there was no way
that this God,
This God they would have me believe in
would allow those things to happen to me
would allow me to be abused and mistreated
would allow me to be tore down,
stripped of my innocence.
I was only a teenager

and I blamed God

I blamed Him for everything.

It wasn't His fault,

any more than it was mine.

But I had to have someone to blame

Or else I might have really believed it was me

--my fault that it happened, continued to happen.

So I let go of my faith,

my beliefs, of everything I knew to be true.

I let go of this God I had grown up loving.

I tried to find a new God

A God that wasn't the same God

-- if that makes any sense

I looked for Him everywhere

I learned a lot of things

about a lot of different religions in this time.

Am I a better person now

because I took the actual time to

research and learn

is my faith stronger

because I questioned it?

Or did I lose out,

did I miss out?

on years and years

of developing my faith

my testimony

because I blamed Him

For EVERYTHING that had been done to me.

Did I turn to drugs because He wasn't in my life?

is that why they became the answer

was that the void I was trying to fill

A void left when I abandoned my faith

Denied my faith in God.

Turned away from Him and sought solace

in the darkest places you can imagine.

"I Used My Agency"

by Amanda Lynn 04/19/2016

God gave me agency, and I took it and ran with it

headfirst into something I know was never part of my plan

They always say you can get addicted

from the first time you use

not sure if that's true,

I don't remember when I crossed the line

Agency means doing what I want, right?

I learned the hard way, that is far from the truth

There are things in this life that take agency away from you

Addiction, I learned, is for sure one of those things

Because one day you wake up

and you realize it's no longer a choice

You're holding a pipe, placing crystals inside,

You're inhaling it into your lungs

and you no longer understand why

It's now a chain, wrapped tight around you

bound so tight, you can't even fucking breathe.

taking it, dragging it everywhere you go-

IT is in control of your life, not you.

IT controls your decisions-

can I use while I'm there?

IT controls your actions-
do I have time to use before I go?
Hold on, I have to stop here-
there's someone here who has,
and I'm in dire need.
Don't care how it's done,
personal preference went out the window a long time ago
have time and a place to smoke it, great.
if not, snorting it with a bill
straight from the baggie will do.
oops. too much, fuck me.
oh well, this is going to be fun.
I used it in solitude,
I used it with sketchy fools
I found myself in the craziest places
surrounded by versions of my past and future self.
those who were just trying it out,
and those who were so far gone they weren't alive.
I can't tell you everything I saw-
mostly it's just too fuzzy to remember.
and if I can't remember that,
imagine what else I can't remember.
facts a mom is supposed to know about her baby are gone
lost in a hazy cloud of drugs.

I'm sorry sweetheart, I just don't remember.

I used my agency to make a choice.

A choice which took my agency from me.

It's crazy how that works,

if you haven't learned that first hand, don't

Please don't. Just take it from me.

Drugs WILL control your life.

From active addiction, to recovery.

To living my life sober

Drugs still have a hold on me.

Want to know how often I craved it while I was high?

Every. Single. Day.

Want to know how often I think about using now?

3 years clean, and it still haunts me

Every. Single. Day.

1,224 days and counting.

this would be so much easier if I was high.

Like an actual voice in my head.

It takes everything I have to shut it down.

laugh at it.

remind myself how not true that is.

Remember: "You can check out anytime you like, but you can never leave."[1]

---

[1] Hotel California, released February 1977. written by: Glenn Frey (Eagles)

That's a scary and sinister thought.

But more than true.

You can use and be sober, that much is true.

You may even return to your life,

as though someone paused the screen

Or find yourself on the road back to Clean

But no matter how seemingly unharmed you appear

It will still have a hold on you, And it always will.

They say you can push it farther and farther back,

the more clean years you have under your belt.

But how long does it take, cause I'm ready to be there.

Yeah, I'm so not banking on that being the truth,

I think I'll just keep my self-imposed rules,

and stay on the road back to Clean.

Telling you all this is tricky.

It's a contradictory story.

I am thankful for all that has happened in my life.

these things have made me who I am today.

But I wouldn't wish Addiction on anyone.

So learn from me, if it's not too late.

And choose for yourself a different story.

"My War"
by Amanda Lynn 02/03/2016

I remember a time, alone and lost

Turning to drugs not understanding the cost

I had my reasons, excuses at best

I thought they beat out the rest

It's a typical story, and only mine to bear

When I was high it was easier not to care

My usual character tried to shine through

But the person I became was foreign and untrue.

I tried to be happy, it was easy high,

And other lies I told myself all the time.

I thought I was better, this superhuman mom.

There was no way any of this was wrong.

Life was great in my fucked up mind.

Blaming others around me when life was unkind.

It's under control, this is what I desire

It makes me better, to this I aspire!

Free agency, I can do what I will,

Don't judge me, this is my thrill!

One day it changed, this mind of mine,

One day God sent me a sign.

Out one night, in a loud club with a band,

Tensions were high she had drugs in her hand.

I got in her face, said don't do it!

You're clean, don't you see?

Just this once, one time, I heard her yelling at me.

One time, is never one time, I yelled in a fit

One time leads to everyday and every day

I wish I could quit!

The words I spoke came from a foreign place

Is that really what I yelled in her face?

Was that the truth? Was that really what I meant?

It was nonsense, right? I thought I was content?

Soul searching, still high I sought the truth after that

I wasn't quite sure I could face that fact

Was this the life I dreamt of while young?

If only I thought this, when I had begun.

I'd lost my life along the way somewhere

It's crazy how I thought I didn't care

One sign after another and I found my resolve.

I would not give up, my life I would solve.

It wasn't the next day, or that night

But I wasn't giving up, I was learning to fight.

Face my demons and take charge of my life

I fought long and hard, and won, but with much strife.

My life is more perfect, though it is not yet done.

The battles inside me have all not yet been won.

This war is not over, it might never be

I will forever carry addiction inside of me

I have to be strong, be courageous in my fight

And never let my destination out of my sight..

I'm a better person, now that much is true

But I wouldn't wish addiction on even you.

Why I'm not dead is a mystery at best

It's the Lord I thank for helping my pass this test.

Without Him I don't even know where I would be

It was Him, I know it, that night speaking through me

And now He has guided me, down this path I'm now on

I know now that during my life He never was gone

It was in that moment, intense and screaming

That I felt my life might actually have meaning.

And so I will continue to fight in this war inside me

When I take my last breath on this earth

it will be in victory.

I will never forget the lessons I've learned

How easy your life can be taken and turned.

"Self-Medicating"
by Amanda Lynn 04/28/2016

An empty shell
feeling not quite whole,
less of a person
blaming those who've hurt me,
for my state of unrest.
So I turn to you
your promises heard
you fill my cup
make me feel whole again
if only but for a minute
until my cup again runs dry
and I scramble, feeling
to make you full again
to numb the feeling
to silence the fears
I am not worthy
I am not good enough
I am not whole
I am less of a person
but with my cup full
I can be better

I can be whole
I can survive
I can be powerful
it's the only way
I'm better
when you've filled my cup
better than before
feeling pain, feeling empty
but once again you desert me,
my cup runs dry
I scramble, feeling
to fill you once more
it never ends
this need
this emptiness
this desire to be whole
not caring who is in the way
only caring how it feels
or doesn't feel
when my cup is full
and I feel whole.
The circle doesn't end
The need is never satisfied
at first it only took a little

and my cup was full
but then
it took more to fill
it took more not to feel
it took everything to feel whole
to feel complete
to not feel those painful feelings
of being empty
of being a shell
of not being worthy
and the circle continues
the price to fill my cup increases
I sacrifice everything
I sacrifice more
for this feeling
of no pain
when my cup is full.
what price is too much
for my cup to feel full
if only but for a moment
again.
until it empties
and once again I scramble, feeling
to fill it once more

never quite grasping

that feeling

that first time I felt full

the first time you filled my cup

filled my shell

made me whole

it's just out of grasp

I am nothing without you.

Meth fills my cup.

makes me whole

makes me better

so I continue to scramble, feeling

to fill it once more.

"The Answer That Didn't Solve Anything"

by Amanda Lynn 05/18/2016

I was happy wasn't I?

when did it change?

When did it go from

sunshine and rainbows

to heartache and pain.

I remember being happy.

I remember thinking

My life is GRAND!!

I mean,

It wasn't perfect.

I still had things I wanted.

But it was better than before

Better than before I walked out-

walked out of his life

left behind the pain,

the misery,

the deceit,

the drugs,

the life that wasn't a life.

I got my baby back,

I had a plan

I was going to have a good life

what happened?

when did I decide?

When did I start feeling broken?

when did I start feeling empty?

What changed?

When did I turn to drugs,

to make me feel whole?

Like, I know WHEN in my life,

I know the year,

the approximate date,

But when, at what point in how I was feeling?

Did I make that choice?

AND WHY?!?

Why was that the answer,

when it had never been the answer before,

when it had never worked out before.

I'd already been down that path

I knew where it led.

Doing drugs had destroyed my life

So many times before

WHY-

did I think that THIS time

that was the answer??

first alcohol,

then drugs,

then harder drugs,

then controlling my life drugs

And why can't I understand now?

That person I was

Why do I feel this need

to understand

is it because I don't want to repeat those mistakes

Because I know?

that in those weak moments

I am WEAK

the WEAKEST of the WEAK.

Is that my fear?

That out of the blue one day

I'll feel empty again

I'll feel that my life is not complete

And I will turn again to drugs

To fill it,

Even though

right now,

I KNOW.

That was NOT THE ANSWER,

That answer

didn't solve anything
that answer–
made my life worse.

"Going Through the Motions"
by Amanda Lynn 08/15/2016

At one point,

in my determination to quit.

I was sitting in church

going through all the motions

high as a kite

but I was trying.

I sat way in the back.

because I couldn't sit still

I couldn't concentrate

on what the speaker was saying

but I knew I was in the right place.

I wasn't exactly going because I wanted to

I was going because of my little man,

who asked me to.

He was going to church

our friend would take him

and he said to me one day

Mom, can you come too?

How could I say no,

to my sweet little boy?

So I said sure,

and together we went.

Sometime later,

sitting in the back.

fidgeting cause I was high

trying to concentrate

on the talks being given

and failing.

I opened my scriptures.

started flipping through them

reading a passage here and there.

reading things I previously highlighted

when I was a teen in seminary

and had last opened this book.

When a passage stood out to me

before I even read the words

somehow I just knew

read that one.

So I read it.

and cried.

The spirit was so strong

I knew this was another answer.

I already knew I wanted to quit.

I'd already made up my mind

though I had yet to succeed.

But this scripture

made my plan start to come together

Like a piece of a puzzle that had been missing.

What that scripture actually says

the story before and after it,

has nothing to do

with the meaning I got from it that day.

It said very bluntly.

Give it up

and serve God instead.

With all diligence, day and night.

Such a simple yet complex answer.

but I knew in my heart,

in the very core of my being

that this was what I was missing.

It wasn't the next day,

and it wasn't the next week or even month.

But more pieces started to appear

and I slowly and carefully

started piecing my life back together.

Until the day it finally happened.

I relapsed after 2 weeks,

again after a week.

I kept trying.

I was determined.

I relapsed again.

And then that was it.

3 months later I realized.

I was done.

I had done it.

I've come too far, to give up now

I can do this!

3 months was a huge accomplishment.

Then came 6 months.

one year.

two years

and now three.

nearly four.

In fact: 1,342 days and counting.

and I've been serving my God

diligently, day and night..

Since reading that scripture.

(3Nephi 5:3)

"Unrequited Suffering"
by Amanda Lynn 05/9/16

Once upon a time
I used to think I was in love
We had so much fun together
maybe once or twice.

After that, you became controlling
deciding my every move.
You changed my thoughts, my actions,
you sought to control my everything.

You changed everything about me,
without even trying.
you turned me harsh and uncaring,
hurting those I loved dear.

Gone was the girl I once was,
now taking my life for granted
throwing it all away
seeking your elusive approval

And for what I still cannot say

You gave me nothing in return
just the semblance of a better life
A fantasy that was unachievable and out of reach.

I would have done anything for your love in return,
I gave you everything I had to give,
and when you asked for more,
I gave you more.

Why didn't I leave, back when it was new
Hell, I could have left way before that 1st night
But I didn't understand what fate you'd bring
Sure, I'd been warned- I should have heard.

But your allure was strong
Was this choice right or wrong?
With as many told me it was wrong
came more saying it was right.

So I chose you, and sealed my fate
Forever I am now yours
Regardless that my desire to be ensnared
changed to wanting you not.

Those who don't understand may call out advice
Leave, run away, take back your life!
You can always fight back,
for the pain this has caused.

I wish it were that simple-
But the lover I chose was not a mere man
I chose an idea, a thought- a chemical
I allowed a Demon into my soul

I called him by many different names
He was meth, dope- my possible future death
He called me broken, empty, worthless
He promised to make me whole

Now I can't shake him
This demon I've allowed inside
Although I've learned to silence him
It doesn't always last forever

He knows my weaknesses
He remembers how he's won me before
He knows the voice of doubt I fall for
He knows my darkest fears.

He waits, biding his time,

While I build walls to protect myself

But will it ever be enough?

Or will he tear down my walls

and conquer me once more?

"Your Deceptive Perceptions"
by Amanda Lynn 04/30/2016

One day.

I want just one day.

is it too much to ask?

one whole day-

where you don't cross my mind

with your lies

your empty promises

your deceptive perceptions

that once upon a time stole my life.

I've erased you!!

I've tried to erase you.

I've changed my life

changed my goals,

changed everything I could change-

to silence your voice

that screaming in my head

in my thoughts

wherever I go

whatever I do

but it's not enough

when will it be enough?

I keep going

I have to.

I remember what it was like

when you consumed me

owned me

controlled me.

I won't go back

I won't do it.

yet there you are again

reaching

into my thoughts

begging to be heard

you can't do this without me

you're better when you have me

can't you see, you stupid little girl

how much you NEED me...

take a deep breath.

clear my thoughts

clear your voice

silence you for a moment

I can do this.

I am better WITHOUT you.

You cannot win

I won't let you

I WILL be strong
I WILL CARRY YOU AROUND,
BUT I WON'T LISTEN.
I WILL CONTINUE TO SILENCE YOU
every single day.
until a day comes
that you fade into the background
when I can't hear your voice
hear your pleading
your deceptive perceptions
completely free of your presence.
But-
My biggest fear
is that I will never be free
your voice will always be there
taunting
whispering
screaming
trying to be heard
in those weak moments
when I almost listen.
All it took was one time
to let you into my head
and even now

even after changing my life
reclaiming my life
living each day en route to
the best version of myself.
there you are.
way in the back
spreading doubt
telling me lies
your deceptive perceptions
waiting for me to listen.

"My Pre-Destined Fate to Choose"
by Amanda Lynn 05/9/2016

Out of my life of trials and addictions
choices I made, consequences and blessings
came bad things, and good things
so how does it all reconcile?

Was this just the life, I was pre-destined to lead
Did someone choose this for me, or did I choose it for
myself
Did I know I would be strong enough, or was it a risk
or did I choose this myself, during my existence on earth

Is there an alternate universe out there somewhere
where everything was different, my desires more grand
3+ kids, all with one dad, married since we were young
or would I have wanted something completely changed

Would I be the same person
would I still be strong
or would my life be easy
never anything going wrong

I can't wrap my head around it
there's no way to understand
how much of my life would remain to be
If I'd never known the Hell of addiction

I met my husband, the love of my life
had I never used drugs, would we still have met
would my one and only, be someone else
would our path have any resemblance to what it is now

Would my kids be the same
or would that have changed too
would anything at all be the same
or was it destined to happen this way

My point in all this rambling
is simply this.
there are so many things I wouldn't risk losing
to want to go back and choose again

Be content with what I do have
be happy with the product of the hardships I face
Understand that it doesn't matter
who cares if it was fate.

I am who I am, *Because* of my choices

I have what I have now, *Because* I survived Hell.

There's absolutely no way of knowing

But I'm fairly certain, *Nothing* would be the same.

"Something I Learned the Hard Way"
by Amanda Lynn 05/15/2016

Whether you aren't religious or you believe in a God,
Believe this to be true:
We all have agency, and exactly 2 choices in this life
We can choose liberty and life or we can choose
captivity and death.
It is our task in life to understand which direction
our choices will lead.
So use your agency to choose things that will lead to
liberty and life,
or choose the other path, that leads to captivity and death.
The trick is knowing which is which.
The one our addiction tells us is liberty and life,
Is actually captivity and death.

"The Support I Prayed For"

by Amanda Lynn 06/01/2016

The voice in my heart
said you need to know
everything about this man.
I almost ignored it
I was so close
to saying no to his request.
Instead I listened
told him yes.
Took a chance
and went out on a date.
I was in the height of addiction
the cards were all stacked against us
It wouldn't work out-
but I listened anyway.
Get to know
everything about this man.
The feeling was so strong
It could have been a voice.
Next thing I knew
I was falling in love
I wanted nothing more

than to be with only him.

Subjecting him to my addiction

didn't seem fair.

yet he stayed,

stuck with me,

and fell in love with me.

I hated what I was doing to him

Hated feeling that I was hurting him

Or going to hurt him

That this was doomed to hurt someone.

He was so perfect.

We were so perfect

Only I wasn't perfect.

I was broken.

How could he love me?

Why did he stay?

Then one day

Everything clicked

I found an answer

knew what I had to do

Knew that I wanted a different life

Knew that it had to be with him

He was my one

The man who I could grow with

The man who I could raise a family with
So I kept praying
Kept seeking more answers
Starting to plan my "how".
And then he said something to me-
Something that sealed my fate:
I'll be right here,
right here my love.
Just let me know
when you're ready,
and I'll be here.
In that moment I knew,
I knew I could do it.
I knew he'd still be there
when I finally stopped.
When I said goodbye
to the life I was leading,
and followed a better path
my hand would be in his.
I could do this.
That was the hope I needed
The support I begged and prayed for
Standing right in front of me
Making me a promise

He kept.

I love this man.

I love everything

He somehow knew I could be.

"Warrior"

by Amanda Lynn 04/27/2016

I am a warrior- fierce, strong, determined, and true

Some could say the same,

but what battles have you been through?

I've fought a demon that pushed me down

into the depths of hell

I fought my way back to the surface,

but more than once I fell.

They say an addict is weak, if only they knew

The path I chose destroyed the weak,

only the strong make it through.

It made me strong,

but don't follow the path I travelled to get here

Not making it out alive

may end up being the least thing you fear.

"Who was this girl I had become?"
by Amanda Lynn 08/04/2016

I'm so lost without you
Although, I was more lost with you

I thought it would be easier to stay
I thought it would be too hard to leave

I thought I could keep control
I thought I could have it all

I thought I could stay myself
I thought I'd continue to grow

I found out how wrong I was
When it was almost too late to change

But I wasn't sure quite what to do
I was falling apart at the seams

I felt stuck in the hole I dug myself
I wanted to get out, just didn't know how

One day it all just clicked
and suddenly everything made sense.

I knew what to do to get clean
I couldn't believe I'd never thought of it before

Who was this girl that I had become
That couldn't see that God was the answer?

It was almost easier said than done
but I found my faith buried deep inside

and I crawled out of the grave I had dug for myself

"To Miss D; Love, May"
by Amanda Lynn 08/23/2016

I've been thinking about you a lot lately
And the potential our friendship had
You said so many things to me
that resonate with me even today.
If only we had met under different circumstances
If only our friendship had flourished without drugs
would it have been different?
Would it have even happened?
For all the deceit that surrounded the life on drugs
there was some good that came from our friendship
I know this is true, because I know if not,
I wouldn't still care about you today.
I know we are still friends
I believe we always will be
I just wonder if one day we can be closer
Like those days we had before
Only minus the drugs and drama.
I hope and pray for that day
when the drugs are so far behind us
that we can be close again
Because my dear friend

you are special to me
and the real times we shared,
Can't have been for nothing,
though they happened between the drama,
they still hold a special place in my heart.
we got each other through tough times
and somehow made each other better people.
you opened up doors and windows in my life
and helped to create the person I am today.
there are so many things I love about
the person I've become since knowing you.
So much never would have happened
without your presence in my life.

"And all for what??"

by Amanda Lynn 08/04/2016

Life is confusing

Just when it starts to make sense.

It all falls apart.

I worked hard.

I got clean.

I turned my life around.

and for what?

To get sick.

To be diagnosed with a life altering disease.

that I will never recover from.

Awesome.

Fuck this.

The urge to use is strong-

It would give me more energy,

help me be happier,

make me feel better,

like it once did

not so long ago.

I know

that's not true.

but when I'm in bed

feeling exhausted

and sad.

it's easy to think.

it's easy to daydream

the nightmare of using again.

I could make it all go away.

I could turn off the stress

of gaining weight

because my body no longer does what it's supposed to.

I could turn off the sadness

that this depression has brought

because my body is out of whack.

I could calm the anxiety,

I could make it all go away.

fade away into a haze of a semi loved life.

I know it only sounds good at the surface.

but sometimes

I feel like I don't care.

Deep down I know

I have worked too hard

to get where I am today.

I can deal with being sick

I can make it through this depression,

the exhaustion,

I can make it.

I know I'm strong enough.

This is

NOTHING

compared to what I've already been through.

I will stay clean

I will not give in.

Because I'm a survivor.

Right?

"Goal of an Addict in Recovery"
by Amanda Lynn 05/28/2016

Relapse, it's kinda what we do...
Our biggest goal,
Is to turn that statement into
It's kinda what we did.
Past Tense.

"Karmic Retribution or Just Bad Luck?"
by Amanda Lynn 08/01/2016

Congratulations you're clean

now on to a brand new chapter

living life, feeling great

no more dying of heat

no more nervous energy

no more forgetting what I'm doing

no more getting stuck doing things just so

feeling wonderful

loving things I took for granted

like restful sleep

being hungry

remembering things

details and dates, and things I'm supposed to do

then...

waking up one day

feeling exhausted

every day

the feeling was not going away

slowly I was becoming more tired

more and more not like myself

can't stand the heat

but no one else is hot
in fact, it's winter girl,
what is wrong with you
restless body
not sleeping
exhausted every day
what is wrong with me?
2 years clean
and now I'm feeling like crap
almost feeling like I used to
coming down off a high
seriously, what is going on?
I'm too young for hot flashes
too young to be so tired
finally I go see a doc,
what is wrong with me?
it's your Thyroid,
rebelling against you
I traded drugs for a couple of years
of feeling good
finding myself again
picking up the pieces of my life
and what do I get in return
congratulations,

you have Grave's Disease

now you're out of whack

your body feels like it's rebelling against you

Always hot, when everyone is fine,

sometimes freezing when everyone is hot

exhausted ALL the time,

sleep does nothing, when you can sleep

restless energy, but too tired to accomplish anything

forgetting what you're doing,

where you're going

what you were supposed to do

can't concentrate

can't control my emotions.

Depression and Anxiety

are way out of control,

here, take a pill for depression

and this one for anxiety,

don't forget your vitamins,

those are important,

more pills to slow your thyroid

and this one will slow your racing heart,

but it's not that simple,

cause we can't seem to get my meds straight

take too much,

my levels are too low,

don't take enough

my levels are too high.

come on doc, what are you doing?

surgery is the answer he says

that's the last thing I need

because with surgery comes

pain medications

and that scares me

that's where most of my addiction soared...

can I handle surgery and 2 weeks of recovery?

congratulations girl,

you got clean

now you get sick

is this karmic retribution?

I just want to feel like me again.

"Gratitude in Recovery"
by Amanda Lynn 05/03/2016

I am grateful
for life, for the chance
to keep living-
really living.

Being alive
actually remembering
my day, my night
all the things I missed before.

I am grateful
for days I wake up
without that burning
that need and desire.

The way I can
leave my house
in a moment's notice-
no worrying about using first.

I am grateful
to be around others
not worrying: do I look high?
do they know??

To drive and not panic
about the baggie in my bra
the anxiety of what I have to hide
when that cop pulls me over.

I am grateful
for the peace I feel
the silence that's actually silent
not filled with imagined voices.

For the friendships I've made-
an equal give and take
it doesn't matter what I have
or don't have to share.

I am grateful
to have money in the bank
and not the equivalent in rocks
that disappear in one night.

A week's worth of wages
pays for more than one night
of torturous misconceptions of fun
spending money on family instead.

I am grateful
for stories, and the ability to read
to sit still for long enough
to enjoy something as I used to.

To be able to get lost
in an alternate universe
able to snap back at a moment's notice
because this time, I'm lost inside a novel.

I am grateful
for so much more than the obvious
it's the little things
the things I never knew I missed.

The pieces of my life
that I will never again take for granted,
for my family, for the life I've created,
out of the nothingness I had left.

I am lucky to be alive—
and for this, I am most grateful.

"This is How Happy is Supposed to Feel"

by Amanda Lynn 01/03/2017

Recovery ebbs and flows,

they say it gets harder

before it gets better

but it doesn't end there

it's going to get hard

and then better

and then hard again

BUT-

don't mistake better

for easy.

I don't think

recovery ever becomes

easy.

It's a seemingly never ending cycle.

It's the Demon

begging to be heard.

Every time he tells me:

this would be easier

if you were high.

you were happier

when you were using.

or any version of
You can't survive without me.
I have to remind myself
of the truth.
THIS is better,
THIS LIFE.
I am happier NOW.
I was fooling myself
when I thought I was happy then.
I had no idea the extent
of what happy could feel like.
THIS right now, is HAPPY.
I am happy that
my head is clear
and I can fight the Demon.
That I have the courage
to get back up
every time he has pushed me down
on my way to right here.
That I have the strength today
to keep fighting him
That I will not surrender
to his charms,
his lies.

This- is happy,

this fight for my life,

this determination,

this blissful,

clear headed feeling,

is how happy is supposed to feel.

"My Silent Prayer"
by Amanda Lynn 09/02/2016

When I sit silently praying

I am talking to Him, my Savior

of my innermost sacred prayers

I confide my fears

and sort out my ambitions

and of my current direction

through all the triggers

that have come my way

Have I truly faced them

or simply kept them at bay.

Which facets of my life still need work?

And in which am I satisfied?

Is the path I chose to take,

when I turned my life away

from the Demon who lived inside,

the path I'm still on today?

Or have I strayed from that path?

I pray each day that I'm continuing along

on the path I was directed to that day.

Am I really the strong warrior

I believe that I am?

I know what I want

and what I don't want for my life.

My task is to make sure

I never fall into the Demon's hands

Never walk down that path again

My answers are not found

in that Hell I've fallen into before

And the only way I can do that

is to put my faith in Him.

"Sweet Dreams, My Darling Lost Child"
by Amanda Lynn 09/13/2016

The one thing that has seemed
to stay with me through it all
although
I am nearly 4 years clean
actively living this new life of mine...
are the dreams
the fucked up visions
that plague me when I sleep
the incoherent
nonsensical
disconnected
ridiculous
nonsense
of mixed up
mashed up
scenes of a life
where I no longer live.
in which I cannot resist.
the beckoning.
the lure of the poisons
I once thought bettered my life

made me feel as if I was

able to exist.

in a world where I felt

powerless.

I know the truth now.

So why is it?

that while I sleep

deep slumbering sleep

where I am able to dream of anything...

I dream of the Demon

whom I have conquered

over and over again.

my nemesis.

I hear his voice

calling out to my heart

my soul, my very being.

beckoning.

tempting me

with feelings of relief.

he insists that I cannot

resist him anymore.

that I should desire

the life we once shared.

that I was better before

enticing me with confirmations

of my darkest fears.

It doesn't seem to matter

what he places before me

in that life

the life I live so vividly

while I dream

I find myself accepting his offering

giving in easily

to the comfort of his reassuring voice

that everything will be okay

that I will feel better

that this is what I need

just go on and do it

use it

lose it

let it consume you

and nothing will matter

nothing will bother you

nothing will be wrong in your life

not anymore.

welcome home

my darling lost child,

to your former

fucked up life.

————

and then I wake
feeling guilty
feeling the relapse
as real as if it were true.
did I use?
am I just waking up from that stupor?
or was that all only a dream?
just vivid visions of a fucked up
mixed up
mashed up
remembrance of a former life
in which I no longer live...
but only
in my waking life.

"My Testimony, Found."
by Amanda Lynn 11/06/2016

I have such a strong testimony
today
Stronger than at any other
point in my life.
I have a testimony
of trials and challenges
I have had so many in my life
I believe
with all my heart
that the trials are given to us
to bless us.
To help us grow,
and become
the best versions of ourselves
At one point in my life
I lost my faith
because of the choices I was making
the places I was going
the things I was putting into my body
drove the Spirit away.
When I chose to change

my life

and give up the things I had been doing

stopped visiting those places

where the Spirit could not dwell

my life changed

so much.

My faith has grown

exponentially

since then.

I know

I have been blessed

because of these trials,

my life has been blessed.

I have an amazing husband

who has stood by me

through addiction,

recovery,

depression and anxiety.

Through the ups and downs

that have defined my life.

I have an amazing family

that I once took for granted.

That I once thought

couldn't possibly be

a key to my happiness.
I am so thankful
that I am alive
to be blessed with so many things.
I tell my story
and some have wondered
How am I alive?
I wonder the same thing.
How did I survive?
How did I find the strength
to stop
to turn around and find this new path?
How is it possible, that I did not become
that future version of the addict
I could have become?
I know that through the whisperings of
the Holy Ghost
that my trials
these trials
have been preparing me
for the things
I still need to do on this earth.
I don't know what the future will hold.
But I know that I am important

If I wasn't, I wouldn't be alive.
I look forward to the day
when I can look back
to this exact time in my life.
and see how much
I will have grown
from the trials
and challenges
I am enduring
and have endured
today.

"My Small but Impressive Success"
by Amanda Lynn 08/23/2016

My small successes in life
are only impressive
when you see where I've been.

I did it with the support
of my husband and family
without the push from charges or court.

I did it before my life was lost
Before severe charges were pressed
I did it before I was forced to.

I am an anomaly-
Not better than another,
even I don't know how I did it.

"Please Don't Follow"
by Amanda Lynn 10/24/2016

I hear your cries
pleading for help
you'd think I was
your best chance,
But I am lost.
How do I guide
my own child
to not repeat my mistakes
to not venture
down that dark path
into a sinister world.
I can't forget what I've seen
the things I've witnessed
the torment remains
images haunt me
my dreams
my nightmares.
Please don't follow
my twisted path
that led me to
this point in my life

it doesn't have to be
the path you choose.
the pain you can avoid
just by turning back
I fear it's too late,
you've drank from
the demon's cup
tasted the promises
of a glorious life
that will never exist.
How do I help you
to be able to see
to learn from my path
but not take it.
That world is tragedy
heartbreak and loss.
once you've lost your self
there's no turning back
a life of addiction will follow you
for the rest of your life
I don't wish my experiences on anyone
especially not my own child.

"Powerless Against Another's Demons"
by Amanda Lynn 06/19/2016

The hardest thing to watch
-as an addict in recovery
is someone you love
drowning in their own addiction.
what can you do to help?
when all you do seems to enable them
giving them excuses or a person to blame
how do you show them all the things
you've learned along the way?
how do you sit back and watch
as the demon rules their lives?
as they light the matches
that burn all the bridges around them
seeing them all alone
in the midst of the wasteland they've created
all you can do is beg to be let in
beg them to let you help them
yelling, screaming, crying,
heart breaking over and over again
wishing you could take their hand
and guide them through the chaos

steering them along the cliffs
to the safety of recovery.
but there are walls and gates between you
and the key is in their hands.
I wonder during these times
what I did to make it through?
where did I find my strength?
and why can't I give it to them??
The hardest thing is standing back,
watching as they find their own way
falling, stumbling and succumbing-
because there isn't anything you can do.
it has to be them doing it for themselves
letting your heart break for them
struggling not to succumb to your own triggers
banishing your own demons
while they blame you and everyone near for theirs.
Praying, hoping, wishing for their survival
Please God, let them make it out alive
let them see how much better
the other side can be!
all the while battling your own demons
your own fears.
as I fumble for the right words to say to you

I find my strength in your struggle
I hear my own truths
in my own voice
and no matter what I see you do-
I know my truth.
I know where I stand.
I know what I want.
I know there isn't a price I wouldn't pay
if it meant the difference in my survival.
Those are the places where my strength lies,
those are the places where my weapons are stored.
Always at the ready
to defeat my demons.
The hardest part,
is watching someone you love
succumb to their demons
even though they are surrounded by weapons
and people banging at the gates
begging to join their fight
The hardest part,
is knowing, there's nothing you can do
they have to want it first.
They have to be the one to unlock the gates.
Pick up their own weapons, and Fight.

"Oh, Please."

by Amanda Lynn 10/03/2016

(This poem edited to remove excessive profanity, original version
published in e-book version.)

It's such absolute crap

How much hate I feel for you

It seems like everywhere I go

People don't care about my day

The first question they ask..

How's your mom?

The center of the universe

The toxic pit of despair.

How's my mom you ask?

I don't actually care.

I know I should

I almost feel bad I don't.

But when you've been torn apart

manipulated by someone

too many times to count.

Damnit, I should have the choice

of who lives in my world.

I am sick of her ruining my day.

her toxins invading my life.

Even from far away.

How's your mom?

Are you actually asking me this again.

Seriously.

Go ask her yourself

Get told a delusional version

of a fairy tale life

she wishes she led.

Let her tell you how unfair

and how wrong we all are.

Listen to her blame her own kids

for her depression, addiction, and despair.

I'm an addict. I know how it goes.

Quit. Relapse. Repeat.

Until YOU decide to change your life.

Pretty sure, she doesn't really want to

How's my mom you ask?

I'm unable to care.

I'm your trigger, Mom?

Oh, please, you're mine.

"My Mother's Oblivion"

by Amanda Lynn 10/09/2016

My mom is an example
Of why I continue to live clean
Our vices were different
Our addictions nearly the same
I saw my future passed out on her bed
Every time I wondered where she was
And whether I would find her dead
The alcohol became her lover
The meth was becoming mine
I always felt that I could function
On or off, up or not
Her life however
Was a downward spiral into oblivion
She will do everything to numb her mind
She even almost died
You'd think that would be enough
You'd think she would understand
But she continues her descent
Lying, Stealing, Manipulating,
Causing those around her pain
What can we do, that we haven't yet tried?

How can we help her to see?
How can she snap out of her fairy tale
Drunken stupor and see how her life could be?
Quitting meth seemed easier
And yet, alcohol is legal.

"My Reality, Told."
by Amanda Lynn 11/29/2016

I feel like I need
to explain my poems
I feel like you need to
know more of my story
to understand
what they mean
and what they say
but on the other hand,
I don't want to explain
I'm sure that those of you
who need to hear the message
will hear it,
those of you who
understand
will understand,
that this was my process
this was me
working through
processing my triggers
my stressors
my life

my recovery

this was me

no longer pushing the triggers away

dismissing them

putting them into the background

hiding them

burying them

this was me

processing them

thinking about

why I have these triggers

and what I needed

to learn from these times in my life

what I needed to pass on

how I felt

what I deal with.

I know

some of my words are harsh

but these are my feelings

these are true

these are

real

this is how I felt

this is how I feel.

I hope that sometime

in the future

more of these triggers

will fade

into the background

that my recovery

will become simple

and easy.

but

on the other hand.

I don't.

because I know

that if I'm working

every single day

to process

deal with

and understand my triggers

that this

will make me

a stronger person,

make me able

to resist drugs

and that life

far, far into the future.

"Freedom from my Addiction"

by Amanda Lynn 12/21/2016

My recovery story
will never be done
Every day
I travel farther
down the path
always drawing near
to the end
to the day
when I can say
I have won
I have defeated
the demon.
He no longer controls me.
He no longer has a hold.
I am free.

"Amanda Lynn"

Amanda Lynn Simons

amandawroteabook@gmail.com

Instagram: @anOriginalCreation

Made in the USA
Las Vegas, NV
10 February 2022

43670098R00059